Charles Godfrey Leland

Hans Breitmann about town

and other new Ballads

Charles Godfrey Leland

Hans Breitmann about town
and other new Ballads

ISBN/EAN: 9783744789417

Printed in Europe, USA, Canada, Australia, Japan

Cover: Foto ©Thomas Meinert / pixelio.de

More available books at **www.hansebooks.com**

Hans Breitmann About Town.

And Other New Ballads.

By Charles G. Leland.

AUTHOR OF "HANS BREITMANN'S PARTY," ETC.

Second Series of the Breitmann Ballads.

PHILADELPHIA:

T. B. PETERSON & BROTHERS;

306 CHESTNUT STREET.

RINGWALT & BROWN, PRS.

Contents.

Breitmann about Town.

DER Schwackenhammer coom to down,
    Pefore de Fall vas past,
    Und by der Breitmann drawed he in
Ash dreimals honored gast.
Led's see de sighdts! In self und worldt,—
    Dere's "sighdts" for him, to see,
Who Selbstanschaungsvermœgen hat,
    Said Breitemann, said he.

Dey vented to de Opera Haus,
    Und dere dey vound em blayin'.
Of Offenbach, (der *open brook*,)
    His show spiel Belle Heléne.
"Dere's Offenbach,—Sebastian Bach,—
    Mit Kaulbach,—dat makes dree :
I alvays likes soosh *brooks* ash dese."
    Said Breitemann, said he.

Dey vented to de Bibliothek,
    Vhich Mishder Astor bilt :
Some pooks vere only *en broschure*,
    Und some vere pound und gilt.
"Dat makes de gold—dat makes de *sinn*,
    Mit pooks, ash men, ve see,
De pest tressed vellers gilt de most :"—
    Said Breitemann, said he.

(5)

Dey vent to see an edider,
  Who'd shanged his flag und doon,
Und crowed oopon der oder side,
  Dat very afdernoon.
" De anciends vorshipped wetter-cocks,
  To wetter *fanes* pent de knee;
Pow down, mein Schwackenhammer, pow !"
  Said Breitemann, said he.

Dey vented py a pauker's hause,
  Und Schwackenhammer shvore,
Id only vant a pig *red shield*
  Hoong oop pefore de toor ;
One side of red, one side of gold,
  Like de knighd's in hisdorie—
" De schildern of dat schild is rich,"
  Said Breitemann, said he.

Dey vent oonto a bicture sale,
  Of frames wort' many a cent,
De broberty of a shendleman,
  Who oonto Europe vent.
" Dont gry—he'll soon pe pack again
  Mit anoder gallerie :
He sells dem oud dwelf dimes a year,"
  Said Breitemann, said he.

Dey rented to dis berson's house,
  To see his furnidure,
Sold oud at auedion rite afay,
  Berembdory und sure.
" He geeps six houses all at vonce
  Each veek a sale dere pe,
Gotts ! vat a dime his vife moost hafe !"—
  Said Breitemann, said he.

Dey vent to vind a goot cigar,
  Long dimes dey roamed apout,
Von veller had a pran new sort,
  De fery latest out.
" Mein freund—I dinks you errs yourself
  De shmell ish oldt to me ;
De *Infamias Stinkadores* brand,"-
  Said Breitemann, said he.

Dey vented to de *virst* hotel,
  De prandy make dem creep,
A trop of id's enough to make
  A brazen monkey veep.
" Dey say a viner house ash dis,
  Vill soon ge-bildet pe,
Crate Gott !—vot *can* dey mean to trink ?"
  Said Breitemann, said he.

Dey vented droo de Irish shtreeds,
  Dey saw vrom haus to haus,
Und gountet oop, ' pout more or less,
  Vive hoondred awful rows.
" If all dese liddle vights dey waste,
  Could *von* crate pattle pe,
Gotts ! how de Fenian funds vouldt rise !"
  Said Breitcmann, said he,

Dey vent to see de Ridualisds,
  Who vorship Gott mitt vlowers,
In hobes he'll lofe dem pack again,
  In winter among de showers.
"Vhen de Pacific railroat's done
  Dis dings imbrofed vill pe,
De joss-sticks vill pe santal vood,"—
  Said Breitcmann, said he.

Dey vent to hear a breecher of
  De last sensadion shtyle,
'Twas 'nough to make der tyfel weep
  To see his " awful shmile."
" Vot bities dat der Fechter ne'er
  Vas in Theologie.
Dey'd make him pishop in dis shoorsh,"
  Said Breitcmann, said he.

Dey vent indo a shpordin' crib,
  De rowdies cloostered dick,
Dey ashk him dell dem vot o'glock,
  Und dat infernal quick.
Der Breitmann draw'd his 'rolver oud,
  Ash gool ash gool couldt pe,
" Id's shoost a goin' to shdrike six,"
  Said Breitemann, said he.

Dey vent polid'gal meedins next,
  Dey hear dem rant and rail,
Der bresident vas a forger,
  Shoost bardoned oud of jail.
He does it oud of cratitood,
  To dem who set him vree :
" Id's Harmonic of Inderesds,"
  Said Breitemann, said he.

Dey vent to a clairfoyand witch,
  A plack-eyed handsome maid,
She wahrsagt all der vortunes—denn
  " Fife dollars, gents !" she said.
" Dese vitches are nod of dis eart',
  Und yed are *on* id, I see
Der Shakesbeare knew de preed right vell,"
  Said Breitemann, said he.

Dey vented to a restaurand,
  Der vaiter coot a dash ;
He garfed a shicken in a vink,
  Und serfed id at a vlash.
"Dat shap knows vell shoost how to coot,
  Und roon mit poulteric,
He vas copitain oonder Turchin vonce,"
  Said Breitemann, said he.

Dey vented to de Voman's Righds,
  Vere laties all agrees,
De gals should pe de voters,
  Und deir beaux all de votées.
"For efery man dat nefer vorks,
  Von frau should vranchised pe :
Dat ish de vay I solf dis ding,"
  Said Breitemann, said he.

Dey vented oop, dey vented down,
  'Tvas like a roarin' rifer,
De sighds vas here—de sighds vas dere—
  Und de vorldt vent on forefer.
"De more ve trinks, de more ve sees,
  Dis vorldt a derwisch pe ;
Das Werden's all von whirling droonk,"
  Said Breitemann, said he.

Schnitzerl's Philosopede.

VEN Breitmann hear dat Schnitzerl
   Vas quardered into dwo,
   Und how his crate philosopede
To 'm teufel had gone flew;
He dinked and dinked so heafy
  As only Deutschers can,
Denn saidt, " Who mighdt beliefet
  Dis ish de ent of man?

" De human souls of beoples
  Exisdt in deir ideés,
Und dis of Wolfram Schnitzerl
  Mighdt dravel many vays,
In his *Bestimmung des Menschen*
  Der Fichte makes peliefe
Dat ve brogress oon-endly
  In vot pehind we leafe.

" De shbarrow falls ground-downwarts.
  Or drafels to de West;
De shbarrows dat coom afder
  Bild shoost de same oldt nest.
Man hat not vings or fedders,
  Und in oder dings, 'tis saidt,

He tont coom oop to shbarrows ;
Boot on nests he goes ahet.

·· O vliest dou troo bornin vorldts
Und nebuloser foam,
By monsdrous mitnight shiant forms
Or vhere red tyfels roam,
Or vhere de chosts of shky rackets
Peyond creadion flee ?
Vhere'er dou art, oh Schnitzerlein !
Crate saint ! look down on me !

·· Und deach me how you maket
Dat crate philosopede,
Vitch roon dwice six mals vaster
Ash any Arap shteed,
Und deach me how to 'stonish folk
Und knock dem out de shpots.
Come pack to cart, O Schnitzerlein,
Und pring it down to dots !"

Shoost ash dis vort vent outvarts
Hans dinked he see a vlash,
Und unterwards de dable
He doomple mit a crash,
Und to him, moong de glaesses,
Und pottles ash vas proke,
Mit his het in a cigar box,
An foice from Himmel shpoke :

" *Adsum Domine* Breitmann!
Herr Capitain—here I pe!
So dell me right *honesté*
Quare inquietasti me?
Te video inter spoonibus,
Et largis glassis too,
Cerevisia repletis,
Sicut percussus tonitru!"

Denn Breitmann ansver Schnitzerl :
" *Coarctor nimis.*—See!
Siquidem Philistiim
Pugnant adversum me.
Ergo vocavi te,
Ash Saul *vocavit* Sam-
uel, *ut mi ostenderes*
Quid teufel *faciam?*"

Denn der shpirit, in Lateinisch
Saidt " *Bene*—dat's de dalk!
Non habes in hoc shanty
A shingle *et* some chalk?
Non video inkum et calamos:
(I shbose some bummer shdole 'em):
Levate oculos tuos, son
Et aspice ad linteolum!"

Den Breitmann see de chalk-piece
  Vitch riset from de floor,
Und signet a philosopede
  Alone oopon de toor,
De von dat Schnitzerl fabricate,
  Und oonderneat he see :
Probate inter equites :
  " Try dis in de cavallrie."

Den Breitmann shtoot ooprightly
  Und leanet on a bost,   [peen
Und saidt ; " If dis couldt, shouldt hafe
  It vouldt mighdt peen a chost !
Boot if it pe nouomenon,
  Phenomenoned indeed,
Or de soobyective obyectified,
  I'fe cot de philosopede."

Denn out he seekt a plack schmidt
  Ash vork in iron shtcel ;
To make him à philosopede
  Mit shoost an only vheel.
De dings vas maket simple,
  Ash all crate ideés should pe ;
For 'twas noding boot a gart vheel
  Mit a two veet achsel-dree.

De dimes der Breitmann doomple
   In learnin for to ride,
Vas ofdener ash de sand grains
   Dat rollen in de tide.
De dimes he cot oopsetted
   In shdeerin lefdt und righdt,
Vas ofdener as de cleamin shdars
   Dat shtud de shky py nighdt.

Boot de vorstest of de veadures
   In dis von vheel horse, you bet,
Ish dat man couldt go so nicely
   Pefore he got oopset,
Some dimes he go like plazes
   Und toorn her, extra-fein,
Und denn shlop ofer—dis is vhat
   Hafe kill der Schnitzerlein.

Soosh droples as der Breitmann hafe
   To make dis 'vention go,
Vas nefer seen py mordal man
   Oopon dis vorldt pelow.
He doompled righdt, he doompled lefdt,
   He hafe a tousand toomps,
Dere nefer vas a gricket-ball
   Vot got soosh 'fernal boomps.

Boot ash he shvear't he'd do it,
   He shvore id should pe done,
Dough he schimpft und fluchte laesterlich,
   He visht he'd ne'er pegun.
Mit *Hagel! Blitz! Kreuzsakrament!*
   He maket de houser ring,
Und hoped de Schnitzerl pe verdammt
   For deachin him dis ding.

Nun—goot! Ad last he got it.
   Und peaudifool he goed,
Dis day, saidt he, " I'll stonish folk
   A ridin on de road ;
Dis day py shinks I'll do it !
   Und knock dings out of sight !"
Ach weh ! for Breitmann dat day
   Vas not pe-markt mit vhite.

De noompers of de Deutsche folk
   Dat coom dis feat to see,
I dink in soper earnest-hood,
   Mighdt not ge-reckonet pe.
For miles dey shtood along de road,
   Mein Gott ! but dey vas dry ;
Dey trinked den lager-beer shops oop,
   Pefore der Hans coom py.

Vhen all at vonce drementous gries
De fery country shook;
Und beoples shkreemt : " *Da ist er ! Schau !*
Dere ish der Breitmann !—Look !"
Mein Gott ! vas efer soosh a shoudt?
Vas efer soosh a gry ?
Ven like a brick-bat in a vight,
Der Breitemann roosh py.

O mordal man ! Vy ish id, dow
Hast passion to go vast ?
Vy ish id dat de tog und horse
Likes shbced too quick to last ?
De pugs, de pirds, de pumple-pees,
Und all dat ish, 'twould seem,
Ish nefer hoppy boot, exsept
When pilin on de shteam.

Der Breitmann flew ! Von mighdy gry,
Ash he vent scootin bast,
Von derriple, drementous yell—
Dat day de virst—and last.
Vot ha ! vot ho ! Vy ish id dus ?
Vot makes dem shdare aghast ?
Vy cooms dat vail of wild tespair ?
Ish somedings got gesmasht ?

Yea—efen so. Yea, ferily—
  Shbeak, soul ! It is dy biz !
Der Breitmann shkeet so vast along,
  Dey fairly heard him whizz.
Ven shoost oopon a hill-top point
  It caught a pranch ge-pent,
Und like an opple vrom a svitch,
  Afay Hans Breitmann vent.

Vent troo de air a hoondert feet,
  (Allowin more or less)—
Denn *polb*—*polb*—*polb*—a mile or dwo,
  He rollet along—I guess.
Say—hast dou seen a gannon ball
  Half shpent, shtill poundin on ;
Like made of gummi-lasticum ?
  So vent der Breitemann.

Dey bick him up—dey pring him in—
  No wort der Breitmann shpoke.
Der doktor look—he shvear erstaunt
  Dat nodings ish peen proke !
He rollet de rocky road entlong,
  He pouncet o'er shtock und shtone ?
You'd dink he'd knocked his outsides in,
  Yet nefer preak a pone !

All shtill Hans lay—bevilderfied—
Nor seemet to mind de shaps,
Nor moofed, oontil der medicus
    Hafe dose him vell mit schnapps.
De schmell voke oop de boetry
    Of tays ven he vas young,
Und he murmulte de frogmends
    Of an sad romandic song :

" As summer pring de roses,
    Und roses pring de dew,
So Deutschland gifes de maidens
    Vot fetch de bier to you.
Komm Maidlein ! Rothe Wænglein !
    Mit a wein glass in your paw !
Ve'll ged troonk amoong de roses
    Und lie soper on de shdraw !

" As winter prings de ice-wind,
    Dat plow o'er burg und hill,
Hard times pring in de lantlord,
    Und de lantlord pring de bill.
Boot sing Maidlein ! Rothe Wængelein !
    Mit wein glass in your paw !
Ve'll ged troonk amoong de roses
    Und lie sober on de shdraw !''

Dey dook der Breitmann homewarts,
  Boot efer on de vay,
He nefer shbeaket no man,
  Und noding else could say:
Boot—"Maidlein—Rothe Wængelein!
  Mit wein glass in her paw,
We'll ged troonk amoong de rosen
  Und lie soper on de shdraw!"

Dey laid der Hans im Bette,
  Peneat de cider-doun,
Und sempled all de doktors
  Vot doktored in de town.
Dat ish, de Deutsche Aertzte,
  For Breitmann alfays says,
De Deutschers ish de onlies
  Mit originell idées.

Dere vas Doktor Moritz Schlinkenschlog,
  Dat vork ash caféopath,
Und der learned Cobus Schoepfskopf,
  Dat use de milchy bath;
Und Korschalitschky aus Boehmen,
  Vot cure mit slibovitz,
Und Wechselbalg from Berlin,
  Who only 'tend to fits.

Dere vas Strobbich aus Westfalen
Who mofe all eart'ly ills
Mit concentrirter schinken juice,
Und Pumpernickel pills ;
Und a bier-kur man from Munich,
Und a grape-curist from Rhein,
Und von who shkare tisease afay
Mit dose of Schlesier wein.

So dey meed in consooldation
Mit Doktor Winkeleck,
Who brackdise "renovation "
Mit sauerkraut und speck.
Und dat no man shouldt pe shlightet
Or treatet ash a tunce,
Dey 'greed to try deir systems
Oopon Breitmann all at vonce.

Dat ish, mit de excepdion,
Of gifin Schlesier wein ;
For de remedy vas danger-full
On von who trink from Rhine.
Ash der teufel once declaret
Ven he taste it on a shprec,
Dat a man to trink soosh liquor
Moost a born Silesian pe.

So de all vent los at Breitmann,
  Und woonderfool to dell,
He coomed to his gesundheit,
  Und pooty soon cot vell,
Some hinted at *Natura*
  Mit de oldt *vis sanatrix*,
Boot each dokter shvore *he* cured him,
  Und de rest were Taugenix.

I know not vot der Breitmann
  More newly has pegun,
Boot dey say he dalks day-daily
  Mit Dana of de *Sun*.
Dey dalk in Deutsch togeder,
  Und volk say de ent vill pe
Philosopedal changes
  In de Union cavallrie.

Gott help de howlin safage!
  Gott help de Indi-an!
Shouldt Breitmann choin his forces
  Mit Sheneral Sheridan.
Und denn to sing his braises
  Acain I'll gife a lied—
Hier hat dis dale an ende
  Of Breitmann's philosopede.

A Ballad apout de Rowdies.

DE moon shines ofer de cloudlens,
    Und de cloudts plow ofer de sea,
    Und I vent to Coney Island,
Und I took mein Schatz mit me.
Mine Schatz, Katrina Bauer,
    I gife her mein heart und vordt;
Boot ve tidn't know vot beoples
    De Dampsschiff hafe cot on poard.

De preeze plowed cool und bleasant,
    We looket at de town
Mit sonn-light on de shdeebles,
    Und wetter fanes doornin round.
Ve sat on de deck in a gorner
    Und dropled nopody dere,
Ven all aroundt oos de rowdies
    Peginned to plackguard und schvear !

A voman mit a papy
    Vas sittin in de blace;
Von tooket a chew tobacco
    Und trowed it indo her vace.
De voman got coonvulshons,
    De papy pegin to gry ;
Und de rowdies shkreemed out a laffin,
    Und saidt dat de fun vas " high."

(23)

Pimepy ve become some hoonger
　Katrina Baur und I,
I openet do lit of mine pasket,
　Und pringed out a cherry bie.
A cherry kooken mit pretzels,
　"How goot!" Katrina said,
Ven a rowdy snatched it from her,
　Und preaked it ofer mine het.

I dells him he pe a plackguart
　I gifed him a biece my mind,
I vouldt saidt it pefore a tousand,
　Mit der teufel himself pchind.
Den he knocks me down mit a sloong-shot,
　Und peats me plack and pluc ;
Und all de plackguards kick me,
　Dill I vainted, und dat ish drue.

De rich American beoples
　Don't know how de rowdies shtrike
Der poor hardt-workin Sherman,
　He knows it more ash he like.
If de Deutsche speakers und bapers
　Are sometimes too hard on dis land,
Shoost dink how de Deutsch kit driven
　Along by de rowdy's hand !

Wein Geist.

I STOOMPLED oud ov a dafern,
  Berauscht mit a gallon of wein,
Und I rooshed along de Strassen,
  Like a derriple Eberschwein.

Und like a lordly boar-big,
  I doompled de soper folk ;
Und I trowed a shtone droo a shdreed lamp,
  Und bot' of de classes I proke.

Und a gal vent roonin' bast me.
  Like a vild coose on de vings,
Boot I gatch her for all her skreechin,
  Und giss her like afery dings.

Und denn mit an board und a shdore-box.
  I blay de horse-viddle a biece,
Dill de neighbours shkreem "deat' !" und
    "murder !"
  Und holler aloudt "bolice ?"

Und vhen der crim night wæchter
  Says all of dis foon moost shtop,
I oop mit mein oombrella,
  Und schlog him ober de kop.

I leaf him like tead on de bavemend,
  Und roosh droo a darklin' lane,
Dill moonlighd und tisdand musik,
  Pring me roundt to my soul again.

Und I sits all oonder de linden,
  De hearts-leaf linden dree;
Und I dink of de quick ge-vanisht lofe
  Dat vent like de vind from me.
Und I voonders in mine dipsy hood,
  If a damsel or dream vas she!

Dis life ish all a lindens
  Mit holes dat show de Plue;
Und pedween de finite pranches,
  Cooms Himmel light shinin troo.

De blaetter are raushlin' o'er me,
  Und efery leaf ish a fay,
Und dey vait dill de Windsbraut comet,
  To pear dem in Fall afay.

Und I look at a rock py de rifer,
  Vhere a stein ish of harpe form,
—Year dausend in, oud, it shtandet—
  Und nopody blays but de shtorm.

Here vonce on a dimes a vitches,
 Soom melodies here peginned,
De harpe ward all zu stcine,
 Die melodic ward zu wind.

Und so mit dis tox-i-cation,
 Vitch hardens de outer Me ;
Uber stein and schwein, de weine,
 Shdill harps oud a melodie.

Boot deeper de Ur-lied ringet,
 Ober stein und wein und svines,
Dill it endet vhere all peginnet,
 Und alles wird ewig zu cins,
In de dipsy, treamless sloomper
 Vhich units de Nichts und Seyns.

Breitmann in Politics.

I.—The Nomination.

VHEN ash de var vas ober,
  Und Beace her shnow-wice vings,
  Vas vafin o'er de coondry
(In shpods) like afery dings;
Und heroes vere revardtet,
  De beople all pegan
To say 'tvas shame dat nodings
  Vas done for Breitemann.

No man wised how id vas shtartet,
  Or where der fore shlog came,
Boot dey shveared it vas a cinder,
  Dereto a purnin shame:
"Dere is Schnitzerl in de Gustom-House—
  Potzblitz! can dis dings pe?—
Und Breitmann he hafe nodings:
  Vot sights is dis to see!

"Nod de virst ret cendt for Breitmann!
  Ish *dis* do pe de gry
On de man dat sacked de repels
  Und trinked dem high und dry?
(28)

By meine Seel' I shvears id,
Und vot's more I deglares id's drue,
He vonce gleaned out a down in half an oor,
Und shtripped id strumpf und shoe.

" He was shoost like Kœnig Etzel,
Of whom de shdory dell,
Der Hun who go for de Romans
Und gife dem shiniu hell,
Only dis dat dey say no grass vouldt crow
Vhere Etzel's horse had trot,
Und I really peliefe vere Breitmann go
De hops shpring oop, bei Gott!"

If once you tie a dog loose,
Dere ish more soon gets arount,
Und wenn dis vas shtartedt on Breitmann
It was rings aroom be-foundt;
Dough *vhy* he *moost* hafe somedings
Vas not by no mean glear,
Nor tid id, like Paulus' confersion,
On de snap to all abbear!

Und, in faedt, Balthazar Bumchen
Saidt he couldtent nicht blainly see
Vy a veller for gadderin riches
Shood dus revartedt pe :

Der Breitmann own drei Houser,
 Mit a wein-handle in a stohr,
Dazu ein Lager-Wirthschaft,
 Und sonst was—somedings more.

Dis plasted plackguard none-sense
 Ve couldn't no means shtand,
From a narrow-mineted shvine's kopf, .
 Of our nople captain grand :
Soosh low, goarse, betty *bornirtheit*
 A shentleman deplores ;
So ve called him *verfluchter Hundsfott*
 Und shmysed him out of toors.

So ve all dissolfed dat Breitmann
 Shouldt hafe a nomination
To go to de Legisladoor,
 To make some dings off de nation ;
Mit de helb of a Connedigut man,
 In whom ve hafe great hobes,
Who hat shange his boledics fivdeen dimes,
 Und derefore knew de robes.

II.—The Committee of Instruction.

DENN for our Insdructions Comedy
    De ding vas protocollirt,
    By Docktor Emsig Grubler,
    Who in Jena vonce studiret;
Und for Breitmann his instrugtions
    De Comedy tid say
Dat de All out-going from de Ones
    Vash die first Moral Idée.

Und de segondt crate Moral Idée
    Dat into him re rings,
Vas dat government for avery man
    Moost alfays do avery dings;
Und die next Idée do vitch his mindt
    Esbecially ve gall,
Ish to do mitout a Bresident
    Und no government at all.

Und die fourt Idée ve vish der Hans
    Vouldt alfays keeb in fiew,
Ish to cooldifate die Peaudifool,
    Likewise de Goot and Drue;
Und de form of dis oopright-hood
    In proctise to present,
He most get our little pills all bassed
    Mitout id's gostin a cent.

(31)

Und die fift' Idée—ash learnin
  Ish de cratest ding on cart,
And ash Shoopider der Vater
  To Minerfa gife ge-birt'—
Ve peg dat Breitmann oonto oos
  All pooblic tockuments
Vich he can grap or shteal vill sendt—
  Franked—mit his gompliments.

Die sechste crate Moral Idée—
  Since id fery vell ish known
Dat mind ish de resooldt of food,
  Ash der Moleschott has shown,
Und ash mind ish de highest form of Gott,
  As in Fichte dot' abbear—
He moost alfays go mit de barty
  Dat go for lager bier.

Now ash all dese instrugdions
  Vere showed to Misder Twine,
De Yangee boledician,
  He say dey vere fery fine :
Dey vere pesser ash goot, und almosdt nice—
  A tarnal tall concern ;—
Boot dey hafe some little trawpacks,
  Und in fagdt weren't worth a dern.

Boot yed, mit our bermission,
  If de sheutlemans allow—
Here all der Shermans in de room
  Dake off deir hats und pow—
He vouldt gife our honored gandidate
  Some nodions of his own,
Hafing managed some elecdions
  Mit sookcess, as vell vas known.

Let him plow id all his *own* vay,
  He'd pet as sure as born,
Dat our mann vouldt not coom out of
  Der liddle endt der horn,
Mit his goot *proud* Sherman shoulders—
  Dis maket oos laugh, py shink!
So de comedy shtart for Breitmann's—
  Nota bene—afder a trink!

III.—Mr. Twine Explains Being "Sound Upon the Goose."

DERE in his crate corved oaken shtuhl
    Der Breitmann sot he:
    He lookt shoost like de shiant
In de Kinder hishdoric;
Und pefore him, on de tische,
    Vas—vhere man alfays foundt it—
Dwelf inches of goot lage.,
    Mit a Bœmisch glass aroundt it.

De foorst vordt dat der Breitmann spoke
    He maked no sbeech or sign:
De next remark vas, " *Zapfet aus!*"—
    De dird vas, " *Schenket ein!*"
Vhen in coomed liddle Gottlieb
    Und Trina mit a shtock
Of allerbest Markgraefler wein—
    Dazu dwelf glaeser Bock.

Denn Misder Twine deglare dat he
    Vas happy to denounce
Dat as Copdain Breitmann suited oos
    Egsockdly do an ounce,
(34)

He vas ged de nomination,
  And need nod more eckshblain :
Der Breitmann dink in silence,
  And denn roar aloudt, CHAMPAGNE!

Den Mishder Twine, while trinken wein,
  Mitwhiles vent on do say,
Dat long insdruckdions in dis age
  Vere nod de dime of tay ;
Und de only ding der Breitmann need
  To pe of any use
Vas shoost to dell to afery mans
  He's soundt oopon der coose.

Und ash dis little frase berhops
  Vas nod do oos bekannt,
He dakes de liberdy do make
  Dat ve shall oondershtand,
And vouldt tell a liddle shdory
  Vitch dook blace pefore de wars :
Here der Breitmann nod to Trina,
  Und she bass aroundt cigars.

" Id ish a longe dime, now here,
  In Bennsylvanien's Shtate,
All in der down of Horrisburg
  Dere rosed a vierce depate,

'Tween vamilies mit cooses,
    Und dose vhere none vere foundt—
If cooses might, by common law,
    Go squanderin aroundt?

" Dose who vere nod pe-gifted
    Mit gooses, und vere poor,
All shvear de law forbid dis crime,
    Py shings and cerdain sure ;
But de coose-holders teklare a coose
    Greadt liberty tid need.
And to pen dem cop vas gruel,
    Und a mosdt oon-Christian teed.

" Und denn anoder party
    Idself tid soon refeal.
Of arisdograts who kepd no coose,
    Pecause 'twas not shendeel :
Tey tid not vish de splodderin geese
    Shouldt on deir pafemends bass.
So dey shoined de anti-coosers,
    Or de oonder lower glass !"

Here Breitmann led his shdeam out :
    " Dis shdory goes to show
Dat in poledicks, ash lager,
    Virtus in medio.

De drecks ish ad de pottom—
De skoom floads high inteed ;
Boot das bier ish in de mittle,
Says an goot old Sherman lied.

" Und shoost apout clegdion-dimes
De scoom und drecks, ve see,
Have a pully Wahl-verwandtschaft,
Or election-sympathic."
" Dis is very vine," says Misder Twine,
" Vot here you indroduce :
Mit your bermission, I'll grack on
Mit my shdory of de coose.

" A gandertate for sheriff
De coose-beholders run,
Who shvear de coose de noblest dings
Vot valk peneat de sun ;
For de cooses safe de Capidol
In Rome long dimes ago,
Und Horrisburg nced safin
Mighty pad, ash all do know.

" Acaiusd dis mighdy Goose-man
Anoder veller rose,
Who keepedt himself ungommon shtill
Ven oders came to plows ;

Und if any ask how 'twas he shtoodt,
His vriends wouldt vink so loose,
Und visper ash dey dapped deir nose :
‘ He's soundt oopon de coose !

“ ‘ He's O. K. oopon de soobject ;
Shoost pet your pile on dat ;
On dis bartik'ler quesdion
He intends to coot it fat.’
So de veller cot elegded
Pefore de beople foundt
On *vitch* site of der coose it vas
He shtick so awful soundt.

“ Dis shdory's all I hafe to dell,”
Says Misder Hiram Twine ;
“ Und I advise Herr Breitmann
Shoost to vight id on dis line.”
De volk who of dese boledics
Would oder shapters read,
Moost waiten for de segondt pardt
Of dis here Breitmann's Lied.

IV.—How Breitmann and Schmit were Reported to be Log-Rolling.

ID happenet in de yar of crace,
  Ven all dese dings pegan,
Dat Mishder Schmit, de shap who rooned
Acainsd der Breitemann,
  Vas a man who look like Mishder Twine
So moosh dat beoples say
  Dey pliefe dey moost ge-brudert pe—
Gott weiss in vot a vay!

Und id vas also moosh be-marked—
  Vitch look shoost like a bruder—
Dat ven Twine vas vork on any side
  Der Schmit vas on de oder :
A fery gommon dodge ish dis
  Mit de arisdocracie ;
So dat votefer cardt toorns oop,
  Id's game for de familie!

Nun, goot! Howefer dis mighdt pe,
  'Tvas cerdain on dis hit
Der Twine vas do his teufelest
  To euchre Mishder Schmit ;
Und Schmit, I criefe to say, exglaimed :
  " Goll darn me for a fool,
But I'll smash old Dutch to cholera fits
  And rake the eternal pool !' "

(39)

So dey cot some liddle ledders,
  Ash brifate ash could pe,
Vitch Breitmann writed long agone
  To friendts in Germany ;
Und dey brinted dem in efery vay
  To make de beoples laugh,
Und comment on dem in de shtyle
  Dat " sports " call " slasher-gaff."

Dere to—as vash known py shoodshment
  Und glearly ascerdaind,
Dat Breitmann hafe lossed money
  Py a valse und schwindlin friend—
So dey roon it troo de newsbapers,
  Und shbeech do make pegan,
Dat *Breitmann* shtole de gelt himself
  Und rop der oder man.

Boot de ding dat jam de hardest
  On de men dat bull de vires,
Und showed dat Captain Breitmann
  Shtood pedween dwo heafy vires,
Vas, pecause he vas a soldier—
  Von could see id at a clanse—
Dey had pud him in a tisdrigt
  Vhere he hadn't half a shanse.

For ash de pold solidaten
Ish more prafe ash oder mans,
Dey moost lead de hope verloren
Und pattle in de vans ;
Und ash defeat ish honoraple
To men in honor shtrict,
Dey honor dem py puttin em
There dey're cerdain to pe licked.

Boot dis dimes it shlopped over,
Tvas de dird or secondt heat
Dat a soldier in dis tisdrigt
Had been poot oop und beat :
So de Pluc Goats dink it over
Und go quietly to vork :
De bow ven too moosh aufgespannt
Vlies packward mit a yerk.

Now Mishder Twine deglaret on dis
De ding seemed doubtenfull,
Boot mitout delay he dook de horns
So poldly py de bull,
Und shpread de shdory eferyvhere,
Dill folk to pliefe pegan,
Dat Mishder Schmit had *sold de vight*
Unto der Breitemann !

He fix de liddle tedails—
How moosh der Schmit hafe got
For sellin out his barty
 To let Breitmann haul de pot;
Und he showed a brifate ledder
 From Breitemann to Schmit,
Vhere he bromise him for Congress
 If he shoost let oop a bit.

Der Twine ras writet dis ledder;
 For der Copitain Breitemann
Vould nefer hafe shtood soosh hoompoogks
 Since virst his life pegan;
He hat tone some rough dings in der war,
 In de ploonder-und-morder line,
Boot vas hoockelperry-persimmoned
 Mit dese boledics of Twine.

Howefer, dis ledder vorket foorst-rade—
 Mit de Merigans pest of all,
For dey mostly dinked it de naturalest ding
 As efer couldt pefall;
For to sheat von's own gonstituents
 Ish de pest mofe in de came,
Und dey nefer sooposed a Dootchman
 Hafe de sense to do de same

V.—How they held the Mass Meeting.

DERE's nodings in dis vorldt so pad,
  Ash all oov us may learn,
  Boot may shange from dark to lighthood,
If loock should dake a doorn ;
So it happenet mit Breitmann,
  Who in shpite of sin und Schmit,
Gontrified ad shoost dis yooncture
  Do make a glucky hit.

Dey hat sendet out some plackarts
  To de Deutsche buergers all
(N. B.—Dish ish not mean *plackarts*,
  Boot de pills dey shtick on de vall),
To say dat a Massenversammlung—
  Or a meeding of all de masses—
Vould be held in de Arbeiter-Halle,
  To consisd of de Sharman classes.

Now dey gife de brintin of de pills
  To a new gekommene man,
Who dinked dat Demokratisch
  Vas de same ash Repooblican :
Gott in Himmel weiss where he hid himself
  On dish free Coloompian shore
Dat he scaped de naturalizationisds,
  Und hadn't found out pefore.

Boot to dis Deutsche brinter,
  De only tifference he
Petween Repooblicanish
  Und Demokratisch tid see,
Vas dat von vash dwo ledders longer;
  So he dook shoost vot seem pat
To make de poster handsome—
  Likewise a liddle fat.

How ofden in dis buzzlin life
  Small grubs grows oop to vings !
How ofden shoost from moostard seet
  A virst-glass pusiness shprings !
Vant klein komt men tot't groote,
  Ash de Hollanders hafe said :
Mit dese dwo ledders Breitemann
  Caved in der Schmitsy's head.

VI.—Breitmann's Great Speech.

DIS tale dat Schmit hafe *seu de vight*
    Cot so much put apout
    Dat many of his bcoples vere
In fery tupious toubt ;
'Pove all, dose who were on de make,
    And easy change deir lodge,
Und, pein awfool smart demselfs,
    Pelieve in every dodge.

Vhen de mceding vas gesempled,
    Und dey found no Schmit vas dere,
Dey looket at von anoder
    Mit a *ganz* erstaunished air ;
But dey *saw it* glear as taylight,
    Und around a vink dere ran,
Ven pefore dem rose de shiant form
    Of Copitain Breitemann !

Den Breitemann vent los at dem :
    " He could nichts well exbress
De rapdure dat besqueezed his hearts—
    De wonnevol hoppiness—
To meed in friendlich council
    And glasp de hand of dose
Who had peen mit most oonreason
    Und unkindtly galled his foes.

(45)

" Berhaps o'er all dis shmilin eart'—
　　He vould say it dere and den—
Soosh shpecdagles couldt nod pe seen
　　Of soosh imbartial men,
So tefoid of pase sospicion,
　　So apove all betty dricks,
Ash to gome und lisden vairly
　　To a voe in poledicks ;

" Dat ish to say, a so-galled voe—
　　For he feeled id in his soul
Dat de *brinciples* vitch mofed dem
　　Vere de same oopon de whole ;
But he lack a vord to exbress dem
　　In manners opportunes—"
Here a veller in de gallery
　　Gry oud, oonkindly, " Shpoons !"

Und dere der Breitmann goppled him :
　　" If *shpoons* our modifes pe,
Dere's not a man pefore oos
　　Who lossed a shpoon by me :
Far rader had I gife you all
　　A shpoons to eaten mit,　·
*Und I hope to get a ladle for
　　Mine friendt, der Mishder Schmit.*"

Dis fetch das Haus like doonder—
  It raised der teufel's dust,
Und for sefen-lefen minudes
  Dey ooplauded on a bust ;
Und de blokes dat dinked of hedgin
  Saw a ring as round as O ;
So dey boked cash oder in de rips,
  Und said, " I dold you so !"

For dis d'lusion to de ladle
  Vas as glear ash city milk,
Und drawd it on de beoples
  So vine ash flossen silk,
Dat Hans und Schmit vere rollin locks,
  Und de locks were ready cut ;
Only Breitmann hafe de liddle end,
  Und Schmitsy dake de butt !

Den Breitemann he crack onward :
  " If any 'lightened man
Will seeken in his Bibel,
  He'll find dat a publican
Is a barty ash sells lager ;
  Und das ding is ferry blain,
Dat a *re*-publican ish von
  Who sells id 'gain und 'gain.

" Now since dat I sells lager,
    I gant agreen mit
De demprance brinciples I hear
    Distriputet to Schmit;
Boot dis I dells you vairly,
    Und no one to teseife—
If I were Schmit, I'd pliefen
    Shoost vot der Schmit peliefe.

" And to mine Sherman, liperal friends
    I might mention in dis sbpot
Dat I hear an oonfoundet rumor
    Dat der Schmit peliefe in Gott;
Und also dat he coes to shoorsh—
    Mit a prayer-book for salfadion :
I vould not for die welt say dings
    To hoort his repudadion.

" Und nodin is more likely
    Dat it all a shlander pe,
So also de rumor dat ven young
    He shtoody divinidy :
I myself, ash a publican,
    Moost pe a sinner by fate,
Und in dis sense I denounce myself
    Ash Re-publi-candidate !

" Und dat ve may meed in gommon,
  I declare here in dis hall—
Und I shvears mineself to hold to it,
  Fotefer may pefall—
Dat any man who gifes me his fote—
  Votevefer his boledicks pe—
Shall alfays pe regartet
  Ash bolidigal friendt py me."

(Dis voonderfol condescension
  Pring down drementous applause,
Und dose who catch de nodion
  Gife most derriple hooraws ;
Eshbecially some Amerigans
  Ash vas shtaudin near de door,
Und who in all deir leben long
  Nefer heard so moosh sense pefore.)

" Dese ish de brincibles I holts,
  And dose in vitch I run :
Dey ish fixed firm and immutaple
  Ash te course of de 'ternal sun :
Boot if you ton't abbrove of dem—
  Blease nodice vot I say—
I shall only pe too happy
  To alder dem right afay.

" Und unto my Demogratic friendts
   I vould very glearly shtate—
Since dis useless mit oop-geclearéd minds
   To hold a long depate—
Dat dere's no man in de cidy
   Dat sells besser liquor ash I,
Und I shtand de treadts *free-gradis*
   Vhenefer mine friendts ish try.

" *Ad finem*—in de ende—
   I moost mendion do you all,
Dat a dootzen parrels of lager bier
   Ish a-gomin to dis hall :
Dere ish none of mine own barty here,
   Boot we'll do mitout deir helfs ;
Und I kess, on de whole, 'twill pe shoost so goot,
   If ve trink it all ourselfs."

Soosh drementous up-loudation
   Pefore was nefer seen,
Ash dey shvored dat Copitau Breitmann
   Vas a brick-pat, and no sardine ;
Und dey trinked demselfs besoffen,
   Sayin, " Hope you wird sookceed !"—
De nexter theil will pe de ent
   Of dis historisch lied.

VII.—The Author Asserts the Vast Intellectual Superiority of Germans to Americans.

D ERE's a liddle fact in hishdory
   Vich few hafe oonderstand—
   Dat de Deutschers are, *de jure,*
De owners of dis land ;
Und I brides mineself unspeakbarly
   Dat I foorst make be-known
De primordial cause dat Columpus
   Vas derivet from Cologne ;

For ash his name vas Colon,
   It fisibly does shine
Dat his elders are geboren been
   In Co-logne on der Rhein ;
Und Colonia pein a colony,
   It sehr bemarkbar ist
Dat Columbus in America
   Was der firster colonist.

Und ash Columbus is a tofe,
   Id is wort de drople to mark
Dat a bidgeon foorst tiscofered land
   A-vlyin from de ark ; ·
Und shtill wider—in de peginnin,
   Mitout de leastest toubt,
A tofe vas vly ofer de wassers
   Und pring de vorldt herout.

Ash mine goot oldt teacher der Kreutzer
To me tid often shb'eak,
De mythus of name rebeats idself
(Vich ve see in his *Symbolik*);
So also de name America,
If ve a liddle look,
Vas coom from de oldt King Emerich
In de Deutsche *Heldenbuch*.

Und id vas from dat very *Heldenbuch*—
How voonderful id run !—
Dat I shdole de "Song of Hildebrand,
Or der Vater und der Son,"
Und dishtripute it to Breitmann,
For a reason vitch now ish plain,
Dat dis Sagen-Cyclus, full-endet,
Pring me round to der Hans again !

Dese laws of un-endly un-wigglin
Ish so teep und broad und tall
Dat nopody boot a Deutscher
Have a het to versteh dem at all ;
Und should I write mine dinks all oud,
I ton't peliefe, indeed,
Dat I mineself vould versteh de half
Of dis here Breitmannslied.

Ash de Hegel say of his system,
  Dat only von maus knew
Vot der teufel id meandt, und *he* could't tell;
  Und der Jean Paul Richter too,
Who said, " Gott knows I meant somedings
  When foorst dis buch I writ,
Boot Gott only wise vot de buch means now,
  Vor I have vergotten it."

And all of dis be-wises
  So blain ash de face on your nose,
Dat der Deutscher hafe efen more intellects,
  Dan he himself soopose ;
Und his tifference mit de over-again vorldt,
  Ash I really do soospect,
Ish dat oder volk hafe more *soopose*,
  Und lesser intellect.

Yet ooprightly I gonfess it—
  Mitout ashkin vhy or vhence—
Dere ish also dimes vhen Amerigans
  Hafe ge-shown sharp-pointed sense ;
Und a fery outsigned example
  Of genius in dis line
Vas dishblayed in dis elegdion
  Py Mishder Hiram Twine.

VIII.—Showing How Mr. Hiram Twine "Played off" on Smith.

VIDE LICET : Dere vas a fillage
　　Whose vode alone vouldt pe
　　Apout enoof to elegdt a man,
　Und gife a mayority;
So de von who couldt scoop dis seddlement
　Vould make a pully hit ;
Boot dough dey vere Deutschers, von und all,
　Dey all go von on Schmit.

Now it happenet to gome to bass
　Dat in dis liddle town
De Deutsch vas all exshpegdin
　Dat Mishder Schmit coom down,
His brinciples to fore-setzen
　Und his idées to deach,
(Dat is, fix oop de brifate pargains)
　Und telifer a pooblic sbeech.

Now Twine vas a gyrotwistive cuss,
　Ash blainly ish peen shown,
Und vas alfays an out-findin
　Votefer might pe known ;
Und mit some of his circums windles
　He fix de matter so
Dat he'd pe himself at dis meetin
　And see how dings vas go.

(54)

Oh shtrangely in dis leben
 De dings kits vorked apout!
Oh voonderly Fortuna
 Makes toorn us insite out!
Oh sinkular de luck-wheel rolls!
 Dis liddle meeding dere
Fixt Twine *ad perpendiculum*—
 Shoost suit him to a hair!

Now it hoppenit on dis efenin
 De Deutschers, von und all,
Vere avaitin mit impatience
 De openin of de ball;
Und de shates of nite vere fallin
 Und de shdars begin to plink,
Und dey vish dat Schmit vouldt hoorry,
 For d'vas dime to dake a trink.

Dey hear some hoofs a-dramplin,
 Und dey saw, und dinked dey knowed,
Der bretty greature coomin,
 On his horse along de road;
Und ash he ride town in-ward
 De likeness vas so plain
Dey donnered out, " Hooray for Schmit!"
 Enough to make it rain.

Der Twine vas shtart like plazes;
  Boot oopshtartcd too his wit,
Und he dinks, " Great Turnips ! what if I
  Could bass for Colonel Schmit?
Gaul dern my heels ! *I'll do it,*
  Und go the total swine !
Oh, Soap-balls ! what a chance !" said dis
  Dissembulatin Twine.

Den 'twas " Willkomm ! willkomm, Mishder
    Schmit !"
  Ringsroom on efery site ;
Und " First-rate ! How dy-do yourself?"
  Der Hiram Twine replied.
Dey ashk him, " Come und dake a trink ?"
  But dey find it mighdy queer
Ven Twine informs dem none boot hogs
  Vould trink dat shtinkin bier ;

Dat all lager vas nodings boot boison ;
  Und ash for Sherman wein,
He dinks it vas erfounden
  Exshbressly for Sherman schwein ;
Dat he himself vas a demperanceler—
  Dat he gloria in de name ;
Und atfisc dem all, for tecency's sake,
  To go und do de same.

Dese bemarks among de Deutschers
　　Vere apout ash vell receife
Ash a cats in a game of den-bins,
　　Ash you may of coorse peliefe :
De heat of de reception
　　Vent down a dootzen tegrees,
Und in place of hurraws dere vas only heardt
　　De rooslin of de drees.

Und so in solemn stille
　　Dey scorched him to de hall,
Vhere he maket de oradion
　　Vitch vas so moosh to blease dem all ;
Und dis vay he pegin it :
　　" Pefore I furder go,
I vish dat my obinions
　　You puddin-het Dootch should know.

" Und ere I norate to you,
　　I think it only fair
We should oonderstand each other
　　Prezactly, chunk and square.
Dere are boints on vhich ve tisagree,
　　And I will plank de facts—
I don't go round slanganderin
　　My friendts pehind deir packs.

" So I beg you dake it easy
   If on de raw I touch,
Vhen I say I can't apide de sound
   Of your groontin, shi-shing Dutch.
Should I in the Legisladure
   As your slumgullion shtand.
I'll have a bill forbidding Dutch
   Troo all dis 'versal land.

"Should a husband talk it to his frau,
   To deat' he should pe led ;
If a mutter breat' it to her shild,
   I'd bunch her in de head ;
Und I'm sure dat none vill atfocate
   Ids use in public schools,
Oonless dey're peastly, nashdy, prutal,
   Sauerkraut-catin vools.

Here Mishder Twine, to gadder breat,
   Shoost make a liddle pause,
Und see sechs hundert gapin eyes,
   Sechs hundert shdarin chaws,
Dey shtanden erstarrt like frozen ;
   Von faindly dried to hiss;
Und von set : " Ish it shleeps I'm treamin ?
   Gottausend! vat ish dis ?"

Twine keptet von eye on de vindow,
  Boot poldly went abet:
" Of your oder shtinkin hobits
  No vordt needt hier pe set.
Shtop goozlin bier—shtop shmokin bipes—
  Shtop rootin in de mire ;
Und shoost *un-Dutchify* yourselfs :
  Dat's all dat I require."

Und *denn* dere coomed a shindy
  Ash if de shky hat trop:
" Trow him mit ecks, py doonder !
  Go shlog him on de kop !
Hei! Shoot him mit a powie-knifes ;
  Go for him, ganz and gar !
Shoost tar him mit some fedders !
  Led's fedder him mit tar!"

Sooch a teufel's row of furie
  Vas nefer oop-kickt before:
Soom roosh to on-climb de blatform—
  Soom hoory to fasten te toor :
Von veller vired his refolfer,
  Boot de pullet missed her mark:
She coot de cort of de shandelier :
  It vell, und de hall vas tark !

Oh vell was it for Hiram Twine
  Dat nimply he couldt shoomp;
Und vell dat he light on a misthauf,
  Und nefer feel de boomp;
Und vell for him dat his goot cray horse
  Shtood sattled shoost outside;
Und vell dat in an augenblick
  He vas off on a teufel's ride.

Bang! bang! de sharp pistolen shots
  Vent pipin py his ear,
Boot he tortled oop de barrick road
  Like any mountain deer :
Dey trowed der Hiram Twine mit shteins,
  But dey only could be-mark
Von climpse of his vhite obercoadt,
  Und a clotterin in de tark.

So dey all versembled togeder,
  Ein ander to sprechen mit,
Und allow dat sooch a rede
  Dey nefer exshpegd from Schmit—
Dat he vas a foorst-glass plackguard,
  And so pig a Lump ash ran ;
So, *nemine contradicente,*
  Dey vented for Breitemann.

Und 'twas annerthalb yar dereafter
  Before der Schmit vas know
Vot maket dis rural fillage
  Go pack oopon him so ;
Und he schvored at de Dootch more schlimmer
  Ash Hiram Twine had tone.
Nota bene: He tid it in earnesht,
  Vhile der Hiram's vas pusiness fun.

Boot vhen Breitmann heard de shdory
  How de fillage hat peen dricked,
He shvore bei Leib und Leben
  He'd rader hafe been licked
Dan pe helpet bei soosh shumgoozlin ;
  Und 'twas petter to pe a schwein
Dan a schwindlin honeyfooglin shnake,
  Like dat lyin Yankee Twine.

Und pegot so heafy disgoosted
  Mit de boledicks of dis land
Dat his friendts couldn't barely keep him
  From trowin oop his hand,   [poot ;
Vhen he helt shtraidt flush, mit an ace in his
  Vich phrase ish all de same,
In de science of de pokerology,
  Ash if he got de game.

So Breitmann cot clegtet,
    Py vollowin de vay
Dey manage de elegdions
    Unto dis fery day ;
Vitch shows de Deutsch *Dummehrlichkeii,*
    Also de Yankee " wit :"
Das ist das Abenteuer
    How Breitmann lick der Schmit

www.ingramcontent.com/pod-product-compliance
Lightning Source LLC
Chambersburg PA
CBHW021528090426
42739CB00007B/829